Ukrainian War Poems

AF229729

50% of all profits

From the sale of this book

Will be donated in full to the

Ukraine Crisis Relief Fund

<u>*Dedication*</u>

This book is for all the people of Ukraine

who have suffered or lost loved ones

during the Russian invasion of their country

Acknowledgement

This book of poems is inspired by the bravery of the Ukrainian people in
the face of Russian aggression, refusing to give in to bully boy tactics.
To all of them I say 'Bravo, you are truly all heroes'.

About the Author

When the Russians invaded the Ukraine in February, the author along with the rest of the world were outraged. What appeared on paper to be between two mismatched participants could not be further from the truth. The Ukrainian people's army fought back and thwarted the Russian plans. The Russians were pushed back from the capital Kyiv, denied air superiority and their fleet was humiliated in the Black Sea. Now more than six months on the war has moved to the Donbas region where it is currently being played out. The Ukrainian heroics are the driving force behind these poems which I hope readers find interesting and perhaps highlight the courage displayed by all Ukrainian people during this difficult time. All views or opinions expressed are entirely my own which I am sharing with you. David Glenister.

'The glory and freedom of Ukraine has not yet perished

Luck will still smile on us, brother Ukrainians

Our enemies will die, as the dew does in the sunshine

And we, too, brothers, we'll live happily in our land

We'll not spare either our souls or

our bodies to get freedom

And we'll prove that we brothers are of Cossack kin'

Ukrainian National Anthem since 1992

<u>Foreword</u>

The Russian Invasion of Ukraine on 24th February 2022 sent seismic shockwaves around the world.

Europe last saw a land war on this scale over 7 decades ago, when the allies united and defeated Germany, their common enemy, ending the 2nd World War in Europe.

Since then, there has been relative peace and harmony between the nations, with the rule of international law generally prevailing.

Russia, with complete disregard for international law, decided to invade Ukraine (a sovereign nation) and thus began the largest land war seen in Europe since 1945.

Russia was in for a surprise. The Ukrainian nation did not roll over and submit but chose to fight. And fight they did. The Ukrainian Army blunted the Russian spearhead causing it to fall back and regroup.

The war is now centred in the Donbas region, where the Russian forces are vying for control of the Donetsk and Luhansk areas.

The people of Ukraine and their armed forces have performed heroics to thwart the Russian advance thus far.

These poems are dedicated to the brave Ukrainian people who have suffered such loss with such stoicism and fortitude.

I take my hat off to you all. Each one of you are, in my eyes, a hero.

David Glenister

24/06/2022

<u>Contents</u>

No.	Title	Page Number
1	Sabre rattling	11
2	Belligerent Leaders	12
3	Not a war	13
4	Evil Spirit	14 - 15
5	Blame it on the West	16 - 17
6	A Loss for a Boss	18
7	Mother Russia	19
8	Snake Island	20
9	Endangered Species	21
10	Invasion Blues	22- 23
11	Mariupol	24
12	Russian Justice	25
13	Summary Justice	26
14	Sievierodonetsk	27
15	Special forces	28
16	Starvation	29
17	The Leaders	30 - 31
18	Drones	32
19	Life goes on	33
20	Putin the Ogre	34
21	Charity	35

1. <u>Sabre Rattling</u>

Superpowers now all re-arming at pace
Developing next-generation weapons, it's a race
With winds of war now starting to blow
The armies are gathering, beginning to grow

Uncertain times, a blast from the past
It's not the first and won't be the last
With sabre rattling and some huffing and puffing
Do they mean it, or are they bluffing?

Meanwhile, the World watches, it's a ringside view
As we watch the leaders and members of the crew
No one wants to see deaths or eviscerated entrails
Let's pray and hope that sense prevails

Is war worth it? What's to gain?
Nothing really, just a whole heap of pain
A fool's dream, maybe, history is not on our side
'Remember Munich' we all cry. If nothing else, it's a useful guide

2. <u>Belligerent Leaders</u>

Belligerent leaders looking for a fight
Don't care whether their wrong or right

With a country in turmoil, full of woe
Let's blame it all on an external foe

An ongoing arms race and Superpowers involved
The problem is not so easy to solve

One can't be seen as being weak
Better to attack and punish the meek

With hard-line rhetoric that's been heard before,
The world watches on as it prepares for war

With army build-ups along respective borders
Each side waiting for the attack orders

Like coiled springs, the soldiers wait
To attack their enemy and go to their fate

With leaders safe, they stay behind
It's the soldiers they command who go in blind

It's a repeat of history, from times gone by
Remember the winner, and forget those who die

And all for what, the power and the glory
Or an entry in the history book - just another story

Will leaders ever learn 

3. <u>Not a war</u>

According to the Russians
It's not a war
It's a Special Military Operation
Something to abhor

Victims of a conflict – that's not a war
Though many people die
Leaving unclaimed bodies along the way
Where they now still lie

The Russian campaign
To demilitarize Ukraine
Masks the true purpose to recover lands long lost
Accepting their losses – it's worth that cost

With thousands of victims to feel their wrath
Leaving desolation and destruction in their path
It's not one-sided - both sides have bled
Leaving the fallen; unsung heroes now long dead

So, now in armed conflict
Its army corps versus corps
Causing untold destruction, death, and misery
Is that not 'War'

Confused – Oh yes

4. <u>Evil Spirit</u>

An evil spirit stalks the earth
Waiting patiently for human rebirth
Like Hitler before, whose deeds were so bad
These evil spirits make mankind sad

To the spirits, time has no meaning
Always looking and constantly screening
They need a host, that much is right
A human being who is not too bright

The next victim identified
One Putin by name
A dictator like Hitler
Who accepts no blame

No longer German
But Russian, of course
Putin has the power
Of a large armed force

But to become an icon,
A world leader for sure
You need to flex your muscles
Ever more and more

So exactly like Hitler
From years before
He invaded Ukraine
And went to war

A blitzkrieg strike
Should do the trick
With an army of conscripts
Is he that thick?

Now months in, and the war is still raw
Putin has stalled though still knocking at the door
Despite many dead on both opposing sides
Their fortunes change daily with the tides

Now an international leper and a social pariah
A proven murderer and a compulsive liar
Putin still stands belligerent and alone
Intent on grinding Ukraine to the bone

Putin a name synonymous with abject distaste
For causing so much death, destruction, damage and waste
An evil spirit still directing its host
Destroying cities straddling the Black Sea coast

As history repeats itself time and again
The spirits are still there, looking to cause pain
Where will it go after leaving this host
Is anyone's guess, but not something to toast

5. <u>Blame it on the west</u>

The Russians planned
Many years before
To reclaim Ukraine
By going to war

As a pre-requisite, there was a need
To rely on avarice and greed
So, they invest Russian Ruble in the west
And it's up to people to do the rest

With a ready supply
Of cheap fossil fuel
Economic warfare
Was the chosen tool

Creating Gazprom to sell the goods
No one saw the trees in the woods
European countries were not too shrewd
They ended up getting screwed

Like an addict to drugs
The west was hooked
They needed cheap fuel
To balance their books

With Russian fossil fuels providing energy for power
It led to demands increasing by the hour
The west took their eyes off the ball
And that's when the Russians let the hammer fall

Like an awakening bear, a fearsome beast
Ukraine was invaded by land from the east
The west responded despite the loss of face
And punished Russia by putting sanctions in place

Too little, too late, the west was caught like a fish on a hook
They needed the fuel, so still, they took
And with Russian fuel flowing, so did the cash
The sanctions effect was committed to ash

With Russia cash rich,
Money seemed to grow and grow
Along with threats of nuclear woe
The Russian invasion did not slow

And though Russian aggression is ultimately to blame
It was western indifference that lit the flame
Allowing them to unleash warfare not seen for years
On a sovereign nation and causing untold tears

The west collectively complicit in this deed
Now need to atone and supply Ukraine's need
It's a long, long road that lies ahead
Along the way, there will be many dead

And the innocents continue to suffer and bleed
Until the day when Ukraine is again truly freed

6. <u>A loss for a boss</u>

President Putin seemed at a loss
Wanted the world to know he's the boss
To flex some muscle, a little war maybe
Something to make the whole world sit up and see

Well beaten in Afghanistan, so mountains are out
With Syria not sorted and the outcome in doubt
We need somewhere flat and closer to home
With plenty of living space for us to roam

Ukraine will do, we've been there before
Took the Crimea peninsular against international law
A strike maybe, to the Black Sea coast
A quick victory for Mother Russia to toast

The Ukrainians will fold, won't resist so I'm told
Time for my armed forces to be bold
Mother Russia is relying on every man
Attack. Attack, and keep to the plan

Pity, the Ukrainians weren't included from the start
They refused to fold, didn't play their part
A quick victory that never came to pass
The Ukrainian military were in a different class

With Russian losses mounting – they fared very bad
The world asked Putin, ***'Are you mad?'***
'This war is costly, it's a massive loss
All you've proved is your inability to boss'

No longer considered a stand-up bloke
The world looked at Putin as a complete and utter joke
A pathetic leader with no moral base
A blot on humanity and the whole human race

7. <u>Mother Russia</u>

A corrupt, autocratic country
With Putin at its head
Has gone to war with Ukraine
Leaving many people dead

A so-called superpower
With a large army to match
Deliberately flaunts international law
And therein lies the catch

Immune to international outrage
And threatening nuclear attack
They invade with impunity
Without looking back

Though an international leper
With worldwide sanctions to boot
Putin carries on regardless
And doesn't give a hoot

Destroying cities and a whole way of life
Unleashing so much trouble and strife
Along the way committing untold war crimes
To enslave a country in its prime

And all because a despot
One Putin by name
Decided on a whim to invade Ukraine
All part of the power politics game

8. <u>Snake Island</u>

Location is everything
Size doesn't matter
Even a speck in the sea
That the chill winds batter

Snake Island: in the Black Sea, that's where it sits
A rocky outcrop straddled with gnarly bits
Strategically important, a gateway to the west
Russians now occupy it, a true viper's nest

But occupying it and owning it is not the same
Despite what is said or what is claimed
A contested battleground from the very start
The Ukrainian defenders played their part

When told to surrender by a seaborne host
They sent the reply that Ukrainians now toast
'Russian warship, go f yourself'*** was the cry
Though in the end, it was either surrender or die

Snake Island, an outcrop
Solid ground to build
Required by the Russians
To install an air defence shield

But doing this is no easy task to meet
Requiring a ready supply of equipment needed to complete
And hampered by missiles and eyes in the sky
The cost to the Russians has been inordinately high

Now months into the conflict
Possession comes dear
With sunken Russian ships
They have nothing to cheer

And with the strikes being so quick and so bold
The Russians are finding it difficult to hold
A well-named island with a venomous bite
A Ukrainian legend: its place earned by 'Right'

9. <u>Endangered Species</u>

An endangered species
The Russian Officer classes
Who, whilst attacking strong Ukrainian defences
Ended up dying in the waist-high grasses

Those officers that lead the way
Wouldn't live to survive the day
Russian generals dying not one, two but eight
There was a long queue at the pearly gates

With so many Generals dying at the front
The army's drive was suddenly blunt
Whilst the Kremlin looked on for a scapegoat or two
More deaths and disappearances are surely soon due

Losing the top brass one a week at the current rate
Russian morale began to deflate
With troops now worried and beginning to wallow
It wasn't surprising with no one to follow

So, for those officers remaining, a word of advice
Perhaps it's time to try to be nice
For if you continue to engage in war, be sure to take care
Or risk going home, a dead Russian Bear

10. <u>Invasion Blues</u>

The Russian Army attacked from the east,
On paper, it looked a veritable beast
To invade Ukraine, what a piece of cake
They would not find it easy to take
With all three services primed and ready
The Ukrainians watched on, rock solid and steady

The air force attacked first when given the order
Followed by the army crossing the long-shared border
With the navy attacking the Black Sea coast
The Ukrainians must fold – least that was the boast
Three different services, all in the mix
Looked like Ukraine was in a fix

The Russian army went to cut off the head
A bad decision that left many Russians dead
On striking the Ukrainian line
The Russians wilted like grapes on the vine
Even with Generals leading the way
The Ukrainians killed them and made them pay

The Russian Air force lost control of the air
With such high losses, pilots didn't dare
Leaving the land forces to bombard from afar
With rockets and missiles that left a scar
A war of attrition, bombardment by shell
These long-distance snipers sent civilians to hell

Meantime, the Russian Navy, with its superpower fleet
Thought they had the Ukrainians beat
The naval attack faltered and fared no better
The cunning plan was not going to the letter
Courage was not something the Ukrainians lacked
Sinking ship after ship in a coordinated attack

One, the fleet flagship, a battlecruiser
Built for war, it was a serious bruiser
So graceful in looks, exuding Russian pride
Until Ukrainian missiles exploded on its side
Seriously damaged and pretty much junk
It floated a while before it just sunk

So, whilst the Russians seemed a veritable host
The Ukrainians were first off from the starting post
Despite fewer weapons and on paper, not a prayer
The Ukrainians were the ones who really cared
No quick Russian victory, that was for sure
Their pre-war intelligence had been terribly poor

Weeks into the war and a change of stance
The Ukrainians now have a fighting chance
A heroic defence against a much larger foe
With losses causing such Russian woe
And still, the Ukrainians stand tall and proud
Shouting *'Freedom'* so very loud

As the whole world watches, all are in awe
At Ukraine's stoicism throughout this ongoing war

11. <u>Mariupol</u>

Mariupol, a city in the East
Stood its ground against the great Russian Beast
Defended by the Azov Regiment, all up for the fight
Inflicting losses against the combined Russian might

What days before had been deemed an easy ride
Was now a matter of national pride
Like the Spartans and Texans who fought in the past
The Azov Regiment nailed their flag to the mast

Holding down the attackers and doing it with flair
They taunted the Russians – come if you dare
Besieged for months, yet still holding out
They held up the Russians of that there's no doubt

A spirited defence against a far larger force
They saved their country and altered the wars course
An epic, a saga, a legend, a war
The Azov Regiment lives on in Ukrainian folklore

12. <u>Russian Justice</u>

Russian Justice
Has one flaw
They are Kangaroo Courts
That follows no law

Not internationally recognised
The process is blurred
With prisoners guilty
Before being heard

Then given a sentence
To imprisonment or death
Despite appeals for clemency
But don't hold your breath

These so-called judges
So full of hate
Will do anything
To create their own Russian state

Over time they will be judged
As war criminals, for sure
When we the affronted
Get even and so much more…..

13. <u>Summary Justice</u>

Russian soldiers
Now in an occupied land
Are finding life difficult
Due to the Ukrainian stand

With casualties rising
It's the way they are led
They take civilians captive
Literally drag them from their bed

They want information
What they've seen and read
So, prisoners are taken away and tortured
Then shot in the head

One such town, Bucha, by name
Suffered this fate, the very same
With its people left reeling from the dead, they found
The victims cry seems to come from the ground

Meantime Russia buries its head and accepts no blame
It truly has no concept of shame
An international affront to all we hold dear
We pray in time for international justice and something to cheer

14. <u>Sievierodonetsk</u>

With Russians attacking
Sievierodonetsk is the prize
It should be easy
They're in for a surprise

The Ukrainians, though outnumbered
Are a united band
Defending their city
After all, it's their land

The Russian artillery send out round after round
Bombarding the buildings flattening them to the ground
Only then will the Russians dare to enter by force
To seize the city and defeat its defenders, of course

A shattered city with debris all around
With defenders still there holding the ground
The Russians are finding the Ukrainians difficult to beat
It's not easy fighting, street by street

It's hand-to-hand fighting
That is exceptionally fierce
Each side looking for a weakness
For them to pierce

The Russian tactic relies on the force of numbers
Whilst the Ukrainians rely on their leadership and skill
All the while, both sides are looking
For their enemy to capture or kill

A city under siege for days, weeks, and months
A city once thriving - now the main battlefront
A pivotal location to be held at a cost
It still can't be saved and so will be lost

15. <u>Special Forces</u>

A specialist Ukrainian unit

Working behind Russian lines

Risk their lives daily

Plucking Russian goods from the vines

Acting whenever opportunity knocks

They are all experts at opening the locks

Grabbing the goods despite the risk

Darting in and out but keeping it brisk

With Russian Tanks

Being stolen to order

Then put back in use

To preserve the Ukrainian border

Supply and demand

That's the name of the game

To return Russian shells

To kill and maim

These brave fighters

Are a fearsome sight

Who risk being caught

Every day and night

16. <u>Starvation</u>

Death and destruction arrive in many ways
Mainly munitions designed to kill and slay
But other methods though not being direct
Cause death and destruction for maximum effect

Take starvation, for example
On people far removed from the fight
Who are denied wheat and essentials?
And now suffering a terrible plight

With Ukraine a basket, they grow the food
This war has left farming somewhat subdued
And linked to the Russian blockade of ports
Those in need are denied exports

So first, they starve from lack of food
And it'll stay that way until the war concludes
Add to that the sanctions and control of the fuel,
Causing worldwide mayhem that is inherently cruel

With prices rising, the poor are ever more in need
And all because of a war based on greed
So, whilst innocent suffer, and famine develops fast
The world asks earnestly, *'How long will this war last'*

With international stakes so very high
The blame game continues, and the innocents die
With the Russians claiming ignorance, they won't stop or halt
Falsely blaming the Ukrainians; saying it's all their fault

So, let's put the record straight,
It's pretty cut and dried
It's down to President Putin, a single man
To enslave Ukraine is his plan

17. <u>The Leaders</u>

Both are the President of their respective country
Now are war to put it bluntly
What's at stake is a people's right
To simply be free, and for that, they will fight

The Presidents line up like boxers in the ring
President Zelenskyy, 'The New Boy on the block'
Versus President Putin, 'The Beast from the East'
On paper, a Russian walkover, to say the least

Putin, the brawler, goes for a knockout blow
Zelenskyy sees it coming, it was delivered that slow
Missing by a mile, Putin hits thin air
Zelenskyy side steps, he doesn't care

A quick response a punch to the face
Zelenskyy puts Putin in his place
With a bloody nose, it's flowing red
The attack now blunted leaves many Russian dead

No knockout blow as Putin had thought
The whole campaign looks pretty much fraught
Putin shakes his head *'How can this be?'*
'I will not let the Ukrainians be free'

Zelenskyy switches tack, using his diplomatic skills
And calls on the west to supply weapons that kill
A good choice made, and the west waves its wand
Delivering ordinance from across the pond

Zelenskyy now attacks and recovers seized land
As the Russians fall back, a disorganised band
But, with numbers and equipment still on Putin's side
He takes the setback in his stride

First round to Zelenskyy.
A clear winner on points
Putin, though down, is still the boss
The Ukrainians will suffer for this heavy loss

With egg on his face, Putin changes his plan
All it takes is to fight like a man
The Donbas region is the place we'll strike
With overwhelming firepower, they will not like

The Black Sea Fleet will plague the sea
Blockading the ports leaving nowhere to flea
But the Ukrainian fighters still have a bite
And meet the Russians might for might

The cruiser Moskva, flagship of the fleet
Ventured too close and got very wet feet
Launching a missile, and with a bit of luck
The Ukrainians watched on as the ship was struck

Now listing and out of control
The Moskva foundered, and over she rolled
Putin is devasted, such a loss of face
Round two to Zelenskyy, who put Putin in his place

Putin is durable, takes it on the chin
Looks at a map and sticks a pin
Mariupol first, then roll up the front
The Donbas region will bear the brunt

Now death and destruction plague the land
As the Russians slowly advance hand by hand
Its toe-to-toe fighting all the way
And continuous, ongoing, everyday

Though Zelenskyy is leading in the diplomatic stakes
The war itself is anyone's to take
Let's all make sure Zelenskyy wins
And that Putin is made to pay for his sins

18. <u>Drones</u>

Patrolling far and wide
In the thermals, it slowly glides
Monitored from afar by some unseen hand
It checks for targets as it scours the land

Its path and orbit are pre-planned and held steady
Always working and ever ready
Looking down from its heavenly station
Beaming back details and information

This silent assassin, alone in the sky
Is fully armed and ready whilst it spys
Surveying the land that spreads like a carpet
Watching, waiting, seeking out a target

Once a potential target is seen on the deck
It's quickly confirmed by a visual check
A command to engage is then the cry
And it releases a missile sending death from on high

A new kind of war
From those trained and willing
Like operators of a games console
Distanced from the killing

19. <u>Life goes on</u>

Despite the ongoing war
The Ukrainians stand proud
Competing internationally
Free people, not cowed

Ukraine is on the world stage
Making news – almost every page
And not just the war
But elsewhere, for sure

And life goes on
It must run its course
Despite the problems
No room for remorse

And with some notable success,
Especially 'The Kalush Orchestra' who would guess
Taking Eurovision 2022 by storm
A tonic for Ukraine that made them feel warm

Supported by athletes wearing national kit
Flying the flag and doing their bit
And more latterly awarded EU candidate status
A welcome distraction, a brief hiatus

It shows Ukraine, through suffering, is thriving as well
No thanks to Putin. I hear you yell
But life goes on though it's changed for sure
Despite the effects of the ongoing war

20. <u>Putin the Ogre</u>

The Ogre, Putin
With a heart of ice
A monster, a tyrant
Who doesn't do nice?

Regaining Ukraine
To him, a god-given right
He has gone to war
And it's now a fight

With overwhelming numbers
In equipment and troops that slowly lumber
Yet still, the Russians struggle to succeed
The Ukrainians fight hard, they will not cede

With Russian death rates high – who knows the truth
The figures are literally going through the roof
The untold bodies now lying-in fields where they still dwell
Anonymous victims of an exploding shell

And all the while, the Ogre is safe at home
Along with his 'Yes' men and nameless gnomes
Ordering forces to go off and kill
Mainly conscripts who don't have the skill

Off to Ukraine doing the Ogre's will
Killing innocents, a poisonous pill
And all the while they continue to die
With their loved ones asking 'why oh why'

And the Ogre watches on,
Perhaps now not so sure
All the time thinking
'Why did I go to war'

21. <u>Charity</u>

Despite the world problems, troubles, and strife
We as individuals get on with our life

Like Lemmings in groups, we act so bold
Believing everything that we are told

It's the age-old story from times gone by
Some of us live, and some of us die

The journey we take is so different for all
Some find it easy, whilst others crawl

Yet through it all, and it's a societal stain
Those with money stay safe in the main

The ones who suffer, and they are many
Are mainly the poor, who don't have a penny?

So, give a thought to those worse off
As they struggle for life, maybe eat from a trough

We, after all, are in it together
And need to help others at the end of their tether

What I'm saying, with some clarity
If you can, do your bit and give to charity

www.ingramcontent.com/pod-product-compliance
Lightning Source LLC
Chambersburg PA
CBHW041054050726
47599CB00018B/2149